SHANGHAI

THE GROWTH OF THE CITY

SHANGHAI

THE GROWTH OF THE CITY

COMPENDIUM

This edition published in 2008 by

COMPENDIUM

ISBN 978-1-906347-45-1

© 2008 Compendium Publishing,
43 Frith Street, London, Soho, W1V 4SA, United Kingdom

Cataloging-in-Publication data is available from the
Library of Congress

Printed and bound in China

Design: Mark Tennent/Compendium Design

058001

PAGE 2: An aerial view over Shanghai which grew from its origins as a fishing town to
become the world's largest cargo port in the twenty-first century
(*Fotolia 1957705 Szilard Szilagyi*).

RIGHT: Even though the Shanghai has been transformed by modern skyscrapers in recent
years, the city still boasts some exquisite architecture as evident in this picture of the old
town (*Fotolia 500732 Mary Lane*).

Contents

Introduction

Aerial view of Shanghai, looking up
Suzhou Creek
(Fotolia 4842813 Jonathan Larsen).

Introduction

Shanghai is unlike any other city in China, and its history is vividly reflected in its development. Its name means "On (or by) the sea", and, although many other Chinese cities are coastal, Shanghai has the added advantage that it is accessible to and from the Yangtze River, which made it attractive to Western traders. As a result, it developed haphazardly, from small fishing village to town and finally to the biggest metropolis in China.

Because of its cosmopolitan background, it consisted for many years of a number of different districts: the old city, the foreign settlements, the undefined but distinctive areas of the shikumen residences—terraces of townhouses with a heavy front wall with a gate opening into a small courtyard forming a quiet green haven—and the Bund with its row of imposing European-style offices. But since the 1980s, Shanghai has developed at an extraordinary rate; throughout the city splendid new buildings and parks have appeared, and across the Huangpu River, Pudong, the new business area of Shanghai, is a fantasy of high-rise buildings and night-time lights.

Its position at the mouth of the Yangtze and its natural harbour helped to make it an attractive international port from the seventeenth century, but its fertile hinterland meant that it was not dependent upon trade. Silk and cotton both flourished there; and the cotton industry led early mechanization, which allowed for a

ABOVE: **Shanghai name sign** (*iStockphoto 4753585 Frank van den Berg*).

future geared to industrial development. It was also a rich area for farming, and Shanghai has long been known for the quality and variety of the vegetables grown in the region, and for the high standard of food produced. Crabs are still caught in the Yangtze, vegetables are still often brought in from the countryside each morning and Moon cakes are still a traditional gift at the moon Festival.

ABOVE: Fresh crabs
(*iStockphoto 4506768 Norman Chan*).

RIGHT: Fresh vegetables at market
(*iStockphoto 4390728 Loic Bernard*).

BELOW LEFT: Egg plant
(*iStockphoto 2648595 Russell Tate*).

BELOW RIGHT: Moon cakes
(*iStockphoto 1994699 pigscanfly*).

Its cosmopolitanism too has affected its development. Most of the Chinese who originally migrated to Shanghai came from neighbouring provinces and shared a common culture; they were tough, quick-witted, and ready to grasp any opportunity. They were also independent; throughout the twentieth century Shanghai has been a major centre of dissent. Even today many of the makers and shakers in China come from Shanghai, and it is said that, even recently, the Beijing Government has felt it necessary to rein in the city's powers in various ways.

The early days of Shanghai

Although Shanghai was founded in the tenth century, it was a small market and fishing town until a wave of refugees from the north came down in the early twelfth century and increased the population to over 250,000, and it was not until the seventeenth century, as a result of Japanese attacks, that the city wall was built. Although this has now disappeared, a ring road clearly marks where the old city was. By then Shanghai was already becoming an international port, but much of its wealth came from the growing and processing of cotton, so it has always had an industrial economy as well being a centre of trade; it has been the city that has contributed most to the national coffers, and has therefore been able to resist pressure from Beijing more easily than less prosperous cities could.

The arrival of the foreigners

In 1832 an East India Company official reported enthusiastically on the potential of the city as a port, but the Chinese authorities

ABOVE Man carrying cotton (LoC 3b02359u).

RIGHT: Map of Shanghai.

refused to allow foreign ships to trade freely. It was not until the Treaty of Nanjing, signed after China's defeat in the First Opium War in 1842, that foreigners were allowed not only to trade but also to live—with their families—in Shanghai and four other Chinese ports.

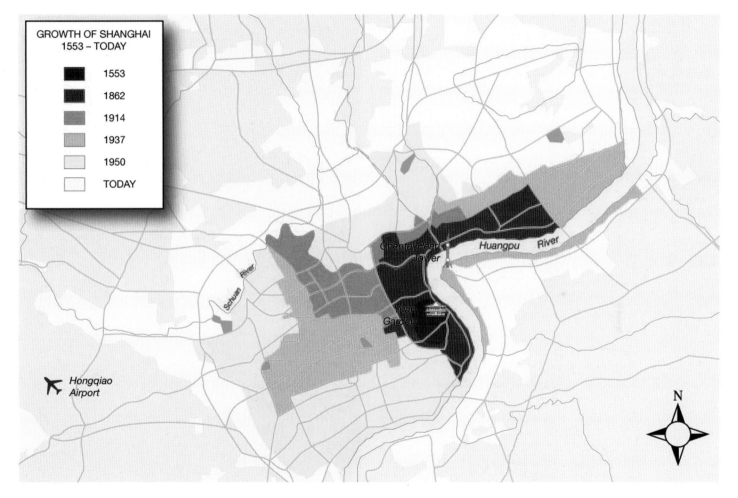

GROWTH OF SHANGHAI
1553 – TODAY

- 1553
- 1862
- 1914
- 1937
- 1950
- TODAY

Oriental Pearl Tower

Huangpu River

Suzhou River

Yuan Garden

Hongqiao Airport

N

They were still not allowed to live in the old city but were allocated land, much of which was marshy and susceptible to flooding; the new residents built embankments, including one on the foreshore, later to become known as The Bund. The water supply was improved, drainage was laid, and the immigrants generally made themselves comfortable. This was the beginning of the foreign settlements in Shanghai, which allowed a variety of privileges to their residents.

With this foothold, many Missionaries arrived, some to stay there, others to travel on to the furthest reaches of China.

The "unequal" treaties

But, in 1853 a branch of the Taiping rebels, the "Small Sword Society", seized Shanghai; as the city authorities were unable to prevent this, the foreigners' Shanghai Volunteer Corps finally drove out not only the rebels but also a party of Imperial troops from the International Settlement. The many Chinese refugees who had fled to the safety of the foreign settlements, were allowed to continue renting property there.

From then on the foreign powers were in a stronger position; the American, British and French residents set up a Municipal Council, and foreign troops allied with Imperial troops to defeat the Taiping rebels.

As a result of the weakness of the local Chinese authorities, foreign consuls took over the administration of the Chinese Customs Service.

RIGHT: The Customs House Clock Tower on The Bund
(iStockphoto 3523944 Terraxplorer/Robert Churchill).

LEFT: A palatial European home in Shanghai *(LoC 3a28905u)*.

Although they remained answerable to the Chinese Government, they were able to increase the volume of foreign trade—much of which, despite being illegal, consisted of shipments of opium.

The Second Opium War led to a further defeat of the Chinese, who, through another "unequal" treaty, were forced to allow foreign ships to trade at ports up the Yangtze, which benefited Shanghai; this treaty also ensured better conditions for foreign residents and traders, as well as a permanent diplomatic presence at the Imperial Court.

Into the twentieth century

This change in the status of foreign traders, along with the vastly increased Chinese population in Shanghai, allowed for the rapid

development of the city in the early twentieth century. Improvements in communications and lighting, the building of modern cotton mills and industrial developments, of substantial office blocks and mansions were all signs of the rapid expansion of the city, and many of them were to last till the late 1980s.

The defeat of the Chinese in the Sino-Japanese War of 1894–5 resulted in an influx of Japanese into the city; they built the first factories and laid the foundations for Shanghai's development as an industrial centre. Foreign businesses and customs, along with foreign vices, made Shanghai a city of wealth and decadence; it was renowned for its culture—film, literature, theatre, as well as high fashion and high life all flourished.

For the wealthy Chinese and Westerners, life was wonderful: for the ordinary Chinese, working and living conditions were appalling; not surprisingly it was to become a centre of Communism by the mid-twentieth century, and was the site of the Party's First National Congress.

The gap between rich and poor, rural and urban, Chinese and Western has long been a problem in Shanghai.

Two worlds, one city

The establishment of the Republic of China under Sun Yat Sen and Chiang Kai-Shek had little real impact on the many foreigners in Shanghai, because of the many privileges allowed to them through

FAR LEFT: Modern high density housing contrasts (*iStockphoto 4185530 Ludger Vorfeld*)

LEFT: with the old houses where many Chinese still live (*Fotolia 3737002 Mirko Humbert*).

LEFT: Chinese junks sail past the *USS Pittsburgh* in 1927 *(Corbis HU029469 Hulton-Deutsch Collection).*

ABOVE: This is the house in the French Concession in which representatives from Chinese Communist cells met in 1921 to form a national party *(iStockphoto 2214758 Zhang Xiao Qiu)*.

extra-territoriality. But the Communists suffered despite their nominal alliance with the Nationalists; when Chiang Kai-shek's Nationalist forces arrived in the city in 1927 to take it over, they killed all the Communists they could find, so beginning the Civil War which was to drag on for 20 years.

There was also constant fighting between Chinese and Japanese forces throughout the 1930s, yet foreigners still flocked to Shanghai to enjoy its sophistication and luxury. More arrived as refugees. In the 1920s and 1930s, there was a large influx of White Russians, followed by the arrival of thousands of Jews fleeing Germany to escape the Nazis.

Later, the Japanese occupied first the Chinese area, and then, after the start of the Second World War, the foreign settlements, and all other foreigners, like the Chinese themselves, suffered tremendous hardships. Even as early as 1927 the Americans stationed the *USS Pittsburgh* off Shanghai in case its nationals were in danger.

Yet until then, to many this was the Golden Age of the city. Even the arrival of White Russian émigrés in the 1920s and 1930s added to its air of romance and intrigue, and the Peace Hotel—with its Jazz band, its Art Nouveau décor and its long list of famous visitors—was perhaps the supreme symbol of this period.

But the Chinese residents were less happy. They resented the wealth and power of the foreigners, and, like the rest of their people, they were humiliated by the Allies' disregard of their interests when drawing up the Treaty of Versailles. This bitterness helped to encourage the growth of nationalism of both workers and intellectuals in Shanghai, who increasingly turned to the Russian Communists for support.

War and stagnation

After the end of the Second World War, China's Civil War continued, but in 1949 the Communists finally defeated the Nationalists and took over Shanghai. Many foreigners moved to Hong Kong, hundreds of non-Communist Chinese were executed, and the city lost its reputation for good living while continuing as a centre for industry; it also continued to make a huge contribution to the national economy at the cost of its own development.

Although its universities were extremely reputable and it was still seen as the centre of fashion and sophistication in Central China, it was looked down upon by the Beijing Chinese, and even in the late 1980s had a rather forlorn appearance. Public buildings such as the Museum were neglected, transport was slow and crowded, and in the late 1980s it was paralyzed by an outbreak of hepatitis. Its glory days seemed to be over.

It wasn't until the early 1990s that it was allowed to invest in its own infrastructure; its speed of development over the last two decades has been extraordinary.

These photos show typical Shanghai scenes in the mid-1980s:

RIGHT: a street scene in Shanghai *(Joan Waller)*;

OVERLEAF LEFT: a typical Shanghai apartment block *(Joan Waller)*;

OVERLEAF RIGHT: and a furniture store *(Joan Waller)*.

The Phoenix of the east

Many high Government officials came from Shanghai, and under former President Jiang Zhemin, once Mayor of the city, the local authorities set out to restore its position as a leading economic centre and the gateway to mainland China. But by 2006 its development was so rapid that the Beijing Government became alarmed, and not only accused the Shanghai authorities of corruption but also appointed a non-native to be Shanghai's Party Secretary.

Nevertheless the city has again become a centre of elegance and culture. Thanks to a change in Government policy there has been much more national investment in Shanghai.

Splendid new buildings such as the new Shanghai Museum, the Stock Exchange and the distinctive Oriental Pearl TV Tower in Pudong have changed the skyline of the city completely. There are large public parks, beautifully planted and immaculately maintained.

A Formula One racing track was opened some years ago. The night sky is a blaze of lights and concert halls while theatres flourish.

Its transport system has been completely modernized and extended. International airports, expressways, superb bridges, metered taxis, a modernized bus service, an efficient Metro, the fastest train in the world and—interestingly—firm control of the number of cars licensed in the city have all helped to reduce some of the strain of traveling long distances in an urban area. But many Chinese still rely on their bicycles!

RIGHT: Yu Yuan—a fine traditional Suzhou-style garden from the seventeenth century *(iStockphoto 3487383 Terraxplorer).*

Yet Shanghai has preserved a number of its old buildings, even if some, like the Yu Gardens Bazaar, have become tourist traps.

The gardens themselves have been beautifully restored: in other areas buildings have been recycled for other uses; many of the buildings on The Bund have changed hands but not their appearance. Many of the traditional Chinese town houses are still to be found interspersed among high-rise blocks. A large number of the foreign-designed mansions and stores are still to be seen, and many, like the Art Deco Peace Hotel, which was badly neglected at the end of the last century, have now been re-furbished and adapted for other uses. Indeed, some modern buildings are pastiches of traditional Chinese architecture.

In its enthusiasm for modernization, Shanghai seems to have been more sympathetic to its past than Beijing has shown itself to be in the mad rush to get ready for the Olympics. Perhaps Shanghai has been more accustomed than the capital to foreign architecture and therefore is less ready to demolish buildings wholesale.

The city of the future

From being a rather drab and neglected city, Shanghai has blossomed out into spectacular colour and innovative design. Pudong, once merely a port for intercontinental shipping overshadowed by the great European buildings of The Bund, has become a Chinese fantasy of glittering towers and sculptured skyscrapers, where magic meets materialism in a blaze of light.

But the size of the city and of its population have increased exponentially over the centuries. When it first became a city, its population was under 100,000; by 1959 it had grown to 5.2 million, and by 2007 18.7 million lived in the city, including two million immigrants or transients, and the city covered 5,800 square kilometers, or 2,239 square miles. Although its population is no longer increasing, demands for better housing have led to an interesting development—the creation of new towns on the outskirts. Nine satellite towns are planned, to house up to 500,000 people; the figures are large, but the vision is extraordinary. One danger is that it is once more becoming one city, two worlds, but the division is now between the rich, whether Chinese or foreign, and the poor—the Chinese workers.

So far, three of these satellite towns are well on the way to completion. Sonjiang, about 20 miles away from Shanghai, is the home of Thames Town, modelled on a traditional English town; at Anting, where the theme is China's latest craze (the automobile), German architects have drawn upon the architecture of Weimar; at Pujiang, 16 kilometers from the centre of Shanghai, there is an Italian-designed city based on the classic grid design of many Italian cities, but interestingly echoes the tradition of many ancient Chinese cities. France, the Netherlands, Russia, Spain, Sweden and the US are yet to produce their contributions, but all nine countries were involved in first, the domination of, and second, the expansion, of Shanghai.

It is as if Shanghai has come full circle, has made its peace with its own past, and is now enjoying being one of the greatest cities on earth—again. But it has not lost its awareness of its own ancient history, and in that lies much of its fascination.

LEFT: A magnificent view of the Orient Pearl TV Tower and the Convention Centre on Pudong *(iStockphoto 4352398 Pedre).*

RIGHT: A lantern outside a shopping mall; red balloons are symbols of good luck and prosperity, and Lantern Festivals are held throughout China on every suitable occasion
(iStockphoto 2376334 fulltopman).

Early Shanghai and the Old City

In China the dragon is a symbol of
good luck; this lively carving is in the
Yu Yuan Gardens
(iStockphoto 4884322 Frank van den Berg).

Early Shanghai and the Old City

Although there was a small settlement here from the late tenth century, Shanghai was of little importance until the sixteenth century. It had a flat, fertile hinterland, so it already had an economy based upon agriculture, cotton, and silk; in addition, many of its residents were fishermen. But because of its situation in the delta of the Yangtze River and on the River Huangpu, it later developed as a port, and in 1553 its city walls were built to safeguard it from frequent attacks by Japanese pirates.

Although the walls no longer exist, the area of the "Old City" can still be clearly seen south west of The Bund, bounded by the curves of Renmin Lu and Zhonghua Lu. Although much of the area has been modernized or turned into a tourist centre, away from the souvenir shops and tourist restaurants it is still possible to find some of the traditional houses, colourful markets and small shops of Shanghai.

One of the main sites here is the Yu Yuan or Garden of Content. In front of it is the Yu Gardens Bazaar; the shops here are not old, but are built in a rather Disneyish version of the traditional style; the zig-zag bridge (said to be the original of the Willow Pattern bridge seen on so much Western pottery) leads to the Huxinting teahouse, built in 1784 by cotton merchants and converted to a tea house late in the nineteenth century. Behind it stands the entrance to the Ming Gardens themselves, a delightful example of the traditional Suzhou

Although now so modern, Shanghai still reveals its ancient past in many ways:
LEFT: goldfish are a popular symbol of good luck *(iStockphoto 3241312 Terraxplorer)*;

ABOVE strange animals on roof tops help to keep ill luck away
(iStockphoto 122645 Kevin Chan); and

garden, created by a senior official at the end of the sixteenth century. Surrounded by a wall and consisting of a series of courtyards creating sumptuous vistas, it contains one of the finest examples of a typical Suzhou rockery. In the old city too is the Ming Chenghuang miao or City God Temple, now small and much restored but once part of a much bigger complex which housed the patron God of Shanghai.

One of the most famous temples lies well outside the old town, to the north west of the city. Jufo Si or the Jade Buddha Temple is well worth visiting, both for its beauty and for its tranquillity in a busy city. Like so much of Beijing, it is not the original building; it was built in 1882 in the Song style, but moved to its present location in the late nineteenth century, and houses two jade Buddhas brought from Burma. South of this temple, on the Western boundary, is the Jing'an Temple, founded originally in the Three Kingdoms Period although the present complex was built during the Ming and Qing periods. It is still highly venerated by traditional Chinese Buddhists.

So much of old Shanghai has been destroyed over the years that few ancient buildings are original, but more recently there has been greater emphasis on recycling buildings and this has helped to preserve some of the nineteenth century buildings which might other wise have been demolished in the city's rush to modernize.

LEFT: a tree of wishes is still used by Shanghai students
(iStockphoto 2412074 yan dong).

RIGHT: Many ancient arts and activities are still popular today; calligraphy is an art as well as a form of writing. Here an expert writes the characters for Shanghai
(iStockphoto 2621974 Robert Churchill).

LEFT: Calligraphy brushes are one of the Five treasures of the Study *(Fotolia 3553121 Rene Drouyer)*.

ABOVE: Mahjong is very popular—the Chinese are great gamblers—but Shanghai has its own version *(iStockphoto 4185085 Jim Pickerell)*.

LEFT: The Chinese delight in miniature gardens, and the growing of Bonsai trees has always been popular *(iStockphoto 3637462 Corinne Martin).*

ABOVE: Silk banners were used to scare away enemies over 2,000 years ago *(iStockphoto 4343782 Hakan Aldrin).*

ABOVE: The roofs were covered by semicircular clay tiles, sometimes coloured and glazed, with patterns imprinted on the final tile
(iStockphoto 1536371 Robert Churchill).

LEFT: And lanterns of every shape and size appear at the popular Lantern Festivals as well as in parks and on buildings
(iStockphoto 4381358 Kinglun chan).

ABOVE: It is difficult to tell the age of traditional Chinese buildings as the same style of architecture has continued for centuries; in ancient times tea houses and private pavilions had the curved eaves still to be seen today *(iStockphoto 4798356 Frank van den Berg)*.

ABOVE: Moon bridges and gates, such as this one in the Yu Yuan gardens, are still to be found in many modern parks and gardens *(iStockphoto 653778 Tomasz Resiak)*.

FAR LEFT: Pagodas such as the Longhua Pagoda, from the tenth century AD, are very typical of Chinese architecture *(iStockphoto 2751370 DesignGeek 1)*.

LEFT: Yu Yuan is one of the most famous Suzhou-style gardens in China and has all the elements of such carefully-designed landscapes; walls surround it but are painted so that they convey a sense of distance rather than isolation. Such gardens were designed by scholars and were based upon a complex theory *(Joan Waller)*.

RIGHT: The garden consists of a series of small courtyards lined by corridors to give asense of space *(Joan Waller)*.

RIGHT: The effect of tranquillity comes from the use of trees, water and rocks, all of which play an important part in the overall symbolism of the garden *(Joan Waller).*

LEFT: From beautifully-furnished pavilions, the visitor sees vistas of the garden framed by variously-shaped windows and doors (*Joan Waller*).

LEFT: Daoism, which is linked with Confucianism, stressed the need for harmony and the search for immortality through meditation rather than action *(Fotolia 442068 Catherine Perarnard)*.

ABOVE: Buddhism, which spread to China from India probably just before the birth of Christ, is still practised by many Chinese *(Fotolia 3551728 Rene Drouyer)*.

The statue of Buddha in Jufo Si, Jade Buddha temple which was rebuilt on its present site in 1918 but closed for thirty years, is brilliantly coloured and surrounded by offerings *(iStockphoto 4481210 David Pedro)*.

RIGHT: Inside the Jing'An temple,
a good example of traditional Buddhist
architecture
(iStockphoto 3903340 Ryan Courtnage).

The Opium Wars and Foreign Settlements

Traditional Chinese houses with carved balconies and curved roof tiles; many such balconies were covered over with concrete during the Cultural Revolution as they were seen as bourgeois. Most of the Old Town was destroyed during the Sino-Japanese war of 1937–45 (*LoC 09939u*).

The Opium Wars and Foreign Settlements

Although little remains of the British and American International Settlement built north of Suzhou Creek, or of the other foreign concessions, there are still many signs of the influence of foreigners on the city during the late nineteenth century.

Trade was not the only magnet for foreigners; many of them came as missionaries, and there are several British and American Protestant churches and schools of different denominations scattered about Shanghai as well as the Catholic Cathedral in Xujiahui, all dating from 1848. The Russian Orthodox Church of St Nicholas is a later addition, built in 1933. The first Shanghai Muslim Mosque, built in 1868, is in the Old City on Fuyou Lu.

The French Concession, which stretches through the South West quarter of Shanghai is still very attractive. Its main street, Huahai Lu, is surrounded by a network of back streets where French mansions neighbour Chinese residences, some later to become the homes of Chinese leaders such as Sun Yat Sen and Zhou En Lai. The "French Park" is now Fuxing Park.

RIGHT: The streets were hung with banners advertising the shops and their goods (*LoC 33558u*).

FAR RIGHT: Life in Shanghai before the foreigners' arrival is still to be seen occasionally. This street scene, although photographed in the late-twentieth century, was typical of streets in the late nineteenth century (*iStockphoto 2209276 Mike Dabell*).

LEFT: Goods were carried along rivers and canals by barges, and complete families often lived on them *(iStockphoto 196072 Dan Chatham)*.

RIGHT: Even at the beginning of the twentieth century, there was little sign of the great European buildings which were to turn The Bund into one of the world's most famous seafronts *(Corbis HU014209 Hulton-Deutsch Collection/CORBIS)*.

This recycling of older buildings has preserved a number of attractive areas; close to Huahai Park, on Taicang Lu, traditional shikumen have been converted into modern shops and restaurants. Despite the pavement tables and chairs, the houses themselves are largely unchanged externally.

The foreign concessions, from the beginning, were better serviced and managed than the Chinese areas; after the defeat of the "Small Sword Society", a branch of the Guangdong Triads, which had taken advantage of the Taiping rebellion to attack Shanghai, was defeated and foreign influence grew much stronger. The Shanghai Municipal

Council, made up of representatives of the British, French and American residents, was given special powers, and the British in particular became agents of the Chinese Government so far as the Chinese Maritimes Customs Service was concerned.

So, it is not surprising that The Bund—built on the waterfront and now one of the most famous sights in the world—was built largely by Western architects financed by Western finance. Some of the splendid buildings go back to the late nineteenth century, others are later, but all of them stamp Shanghai as a quasi-Imperial city, so it is not surprising, either, that, despite the local residents' opposition to foreign domination, it is only comparatively recently that the Chinese have been able to put their own stamp on parts of their own city.

RIGHT: Although the services were soon to be improved in the concessions, life for the Chinese in the old city was difficult; there was no running water so water carriers collected water from street fountains (*LoC 3b02269u*).

FAR RIGHT: Even in 1930 some of the streets looked much as they would have done before the Westerners arrived (*Corbis PG15151*).

RIGHT: As early as 1894–5 there were ominous signs of future conflict with the Japanese, as suggested by the view of Chinese gunboats in the harbour during the first Sino-Japanese war (*LoC3b43422u*).

FAR RIGHT: By the turn of the century, the presence of foreigners was more noticeable; this photograph of 1900 looking across to the French Concession shows a mixed population (*LoC 3a02686u*).

OVERLEAF: An increasingly industrialized harbour is crowded with barges and two-oared rowing boats; traditionally Chinese boatmen faced the prow when rowing (*LoC 3c16669u*).

FAR LEFT: Increasing resentment against the foreigners was shown by The Boxer rebellion of the late nineteenth century; seen by Westerners as a rebellion by ignorant peasants against the Imperial West. To many Chinese, the rebellion was the first sign of increasing Chinese Nationalism; the body of one of the victims of the Boxers is seen here surrounded by French missionaries *(LoC 3c03015u)*.

LEFT: Although the influx of foreigners had increased, many of them came as missionaries rather than aggressors— although the Chinese were possibly unaware of the distinction! In 1901 the Jesuit Orphanage was helping the local population and encouraging converts *(LoC 3b39005u)*.

RIGHT: The aim of the South Gate Presbyterian Mission School was to give children an all-round education. Here the pupils exercise with dumb-bells *(LoC 3b00334u)*.

ABOVE: Even in everyday dress there was a clear distinction between Chinese and foreign residents, as is apparent in this photograph of a Mission school for girls in the early twentieth century (*LoC 3c10735u*).

RIGHT: The difference in dress is even more apparent in this photograph taken in the Nanjing Road in the early twentieth century (*LoC 22594u*).

FAR RIGHT: Foreign missionaries made their mark not only upon the lives of the Chinese but also upon the architecture in Shanghai; a Catholic Church in the city centre still stands out (*iStockphoto 4248214 Loic Bernard*).

The Early Twentieth Century: One City, Two Worlds

Nanjing Road in 1931 contained the busiest road junction in Shanghai; this photograph shows the mixing of cultures in the shopping areas of the city (*LoC 3c10738u*).

The Early Twentieth Century: One City, Two Worlds

Despite the turbulence of early twentieth century China, foreigners continued to flood into Shanghai, and to live lives of luxury. The Republic of China was established in 1912, but the early struggles between Nationalists, under Sun Yat-sen and later Chiang Kai-shek, and the newly-formed Communist Party led, amongst others, by Mao Zedong, Zhou Enlai and Deng Xiaoping, had little effect upon those living a life of comparative luxury in the various foreign concessions.

The foreign population went up rapidly in the early twentieth century, mainly due to the arrival of Japanese immigrants after Japan's defeat of China in 1895, and the influx of White Russian refugees in the 1920s and 1930s and of Jews in the 1930s. Buildings on The Bund and in the various foreign settlements during the 1920s and 1930s emphasize the wealth and high standard of living of these incomers. Many Western traders set up branches in Shanghai, many stores sold Western goods under Chinese names: Tai Kong Canned Provisions, Parker Pens, and, despite the Chinese dislike of the smell of dairy products, the Yah Shing Dairy, are only a few examples of this trend.

But there were other indications of Western influence. The Art Deco Park and Peace hotels were famous for their luxury; the old Racecourse, which after the Communist 1949 Revolution became first a centre for political rallies and later the attractive People's Park and site of the Shanghai Museum and Shanghai Art Museum, was then the centre of Western social life. Prostitution was rife

LEFT: As late as the early 1930s many of the streets of Shanghai were still typically Chinese, but much of the Chinese "Old City" was to disappear as the result of Japanese bombing. This picture of the Nanjing Road in 1932 shows what life was like before the bombing *(Corbis PL5509 Bettmann/Corbis)*.

ABOVE: Nanjing Road in 1934; both these photographs foreshadow the future of this famous road as one of the great shopping streets of the world for both Chinese and foreigners *(Corbis GNAS779 Bettmann/Corbis)*.

particularly in the Fuzhou Lu area; Huangpu Park was notorious for its refusal to allow Chinese, or dogs, to enter.

Although the Chinese had been allowed to lease property in the French and International settlements since 1854 (when the Shanghai Municipal Council had been set up), they led very different lives from their foreign neighbours which would alter the later development of the city.

They had been opposed to many of the improvements which the foreigners made in the nineteenth century, sometimes for financial reasons (the loss of ancestral lands for new railways); sometimes for cultural reasons (the disturbing of ancestral ghosts by commercial and industrial developments). But these had gone ahead despite their opposition. Some local traders did well, but the majority of the Chinese population lived in appalling slums, adults and children alike worked in factories, where pollution and the cruelty of supervisors resulted in high rates of illness and death. Apart from their poor living and working conditions, the Chinese residents resented the extra-territorial rights of the foreigners, whereby they were not subject to the laws of the Chinese.

Although Communism in Shanghai came originally through students and Intellectuals, encouraged by the Russians, it is not surprising that it soon took root among the workers; the house in the French Concession where the Communist Party held its First National Congress in 1921 is carefully preserved and contains an exhibition tracing the development of the Communist Party in China.

But the late 1930s were to bring to an end this chapter of Shanghai's history.

ABOVE: This photograph of Foochow Road in 1931 shows in detail typical Chinese homes and shops of the period *(LoC 3c10737u)*.

RIGHT: In contrast to the foreigners, many Chinese in Shanghai were on the verge of starving. Members of the British Colony issued famine tickets to the poor and needy in 1911 *(Corbis BE081330 Bettmann/Corbis)*.

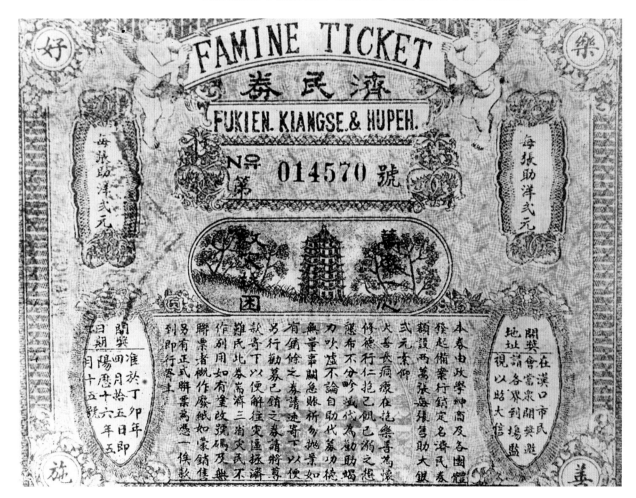

RIGHT: The influx of Japanese traders had introduced industrialization to Shanghai, which was to benefit the city in the long run, but at this time many of the Chinese workers, including children, worked in appalling conditions, although this egg factory of the 1930s looks comparatively well-run *(LoC 3b27201u)*.

FAR RIGHT: This silk loom was still in use in the twenty-first century in a factory set up to attract tourists *(Joan Waller)*.

ABOVE: Much work still has to be carried out by hand. Here, workers pull out the thread of a single cocoon to make a layer in a traditional silk quilt *(Joan Waller)*.

RIGHT: Even in 1935 Chinese labourers were straining to pull heavy loads of silver bullion and other goods *(Corbis GNAS793 Bettmann/Corbis)*.

LEFT: This photograph taken in 1925 shows Huangpu River with factories in the background; in the foreground are the heavily-laden boats rowed by Chinese workers, many of whom lived with their families onboard. The photograph was taken from the British Public Gardens, where the notorious sign No Dogs or Chinese once stood *(Corbis U333675INP Bettmann/Corbis)*.

ABOVE: The difference between the lives of the local people and the foreigners is well illustrated by this photograph showing Chinese women weeding the lawns in front of a luxurious European mansion *(LoC 3a28889u)*.

ABOVE: In contrast, from the beginning, life for the foreigners in the Concessions was extremely pleasant, as can be seen from this photograph *(LoC 3a28906u)*.

RIGHT: Anyone for tennis?—except the locals *(LoC 3b27205u)*.

FAR RIGHT: Social life centred on The Shanghai Club, seen here beside the Canadian Pacific Building on The Bund in the 1920s, where the division between the Chinese and the Foreigners is clearly marked *(LoC 33411u)*.

ABOVE: Hotels such as the Peace Hotel were very fashionable and, by the 1930s, Shanghai was known world-wide as a centre of luxury, decadence and—eventually—vice. Prostitution, drugs and violent crime were rife *(Corbis AABL001698 Jon Hicks/CORBIS)*.

LEFT: It is not surprising that Shanghai was to become a centre of Communism; behind this door the Party's First National Congress was held. The house in the French Concession, where several later High-ranking Communists had homes, is now a Museum devoted to the Party (*iStockphoto 3481117 Terraxplorer*).

ABOVE: On The Bund another of the early Party leaders, Chen Yi, stares down at that symbol of foreign capitalism, having replaced the Western War Memorial (*iStockphoto 2960515 Peggy de Meure*).

The Bund has for many years been one of the best-known seafronts in the world. Some of the buildings have changed hands but, from the outside, its frontage is little altered from when it was first built, although nowadays it is backed by skyscrapers *(Fotolia 4168772 vanostaeten&demunynck).*

LEFT: In the early twentieth century there is no sign of the great buildings which were to form The Bund in the future *(Corbis HU044235 Hulton-Deutsch/Corbis).*

ABOVE: The Hong Kong and Shanghai Bank, said to be the most beautiful building in Asia, was built in 1921 *(LoC 3c10734u).*

RIGHT: At the entrance are the famous lions which many people still rub today in the hope of good luck *(iStockphoto 4149047 Doris Van Ostaeyen).*

LEFT: By 1931 great liners were anchoring in the safe harbour alongside warships *(LoC 3a49261u).*

RIGHT: In 1935, The Bund was still the focus of a vast sea-trade, although nowadays heavy container ships anchor lower down the river *(Corbis GNAS780 Bettmann/Corbis).*

LEFT: Road traffic too changed dramatically. The rickshaws of the early twentieth century *(Corbis H16247)*

RIGHT: gave way to streetcars in the 1930s *(Corbis IH121197 Michael Masian Historic Photographs/Corbis).*

ABOVE: But the Chinese were already at war with the Japanese and, though the life of foreigners was to continue largely unchanged until the outbreak of the Second World War, they too were then to be interned till Japan's defeat in 1945. By then Shanghai's glory seemed to have faded. *(Flag_of_Japan)*

Shanghai in Decline

War comes to Shanghai. The arrival of *USS Pittsburgh* in Shanghai Harbour in 1927 was a sign that, despite the calm of the foreign residents, the Western Governments were ready for an outbreak of violence; China was going through a very turbulent time between 1916 and 1928 as Warlords fought each other all over the country *(Corbis HUO29462 Hulton-Deutsch Collection/CORBIS)*.

Shanghai in Decline

Even in the early 1930s there had been anti-Japanese demonstrations in Shanghai as a result of Japanese attempts to dominate the city, and in 1937 the Chinese dropped bombs on The Bund and on the Great World Amusement Center, which was notorious for the lavishness and decadence of its attractions. During the following five years the Japanese increasingly took control of Shanghai, dominating the city's infrastructure and persecuting the Chinese population, although at first other foreigners were comparatively immune from their attacks. This immunity came to an end in 1943, when all non-Japanese foreigners—estimated to number around 8,000—were interned.

For two years the city was in the grip of a nightmare. The level of violent crime rose, with murders and brutal attacks becoming everyday occurrences. The shortage of food was so severe that it is said that human flesh was being sold and eaten. Japanese bombs flattened most of the city, including parts of the Concessions. Yet, despite all the

RIGHT: From the end of the nineteenth century, China had been going through a turbulent time; there were internal rebellions against both the Chinese Court and foreigners, fights between War Lords, an ongoing Civil War between Nationalists and Communists, and finally two Sino-Japanese Wars. Although the Second Sino-Japanese War did not start officially until 1937, the Japanese were attacking Shanghai residents as early as 1932; here smoke billows from buildings in the Chinese business district
(*Corbis HUO37343 Hulton-Deutsch Collection/Corbis*)

FAR RIGHT: At a time when few people had washing machines or even running hot water, and bicycles were the main form of transport, scenes such as this were a common sight in the back streets of Shanghai (*iStockphoto 4221932 Mark Gartland*).

destruction, a year after the Second World War ended in 1945—even though the Chinese Civil War was still causing chaos in the rest of China—Shanghai's foreign trade had increased remarkably.

In 1949, the Communists finally defeated the Nationalists, and took back Shanghai from the Japanese; the Longhua Cemetery of Martyrs on Longhua Lu was built to honour those who died before this final victory. Despite differences in ideology, foreign investment continued until the outbreak of the Korean War in 1950, when most Shanghai-based foreign companies moved to Hong Kong. But the Chinese Government organized health and re-education projects to help the thousands of prostitutes who were left destitute, and many of the European buildings were taken over by local organizations.

The Shanghai tradition of producing quality manufactured goods, ranging from cars to high fashion, led to its continuing to be China's second city, both in terms of wealth and governance; many of its leading citizens became Government leaders. In addition, the Russians became particularly influential, not only politically but also economically. The Soviet-style Shanghai Exhibition Centre on Yan'an Zhong Lu, built in 1954 and now a huge shopping centre, was originally designed to celebrate China's rapid development since 1949 under Communist rule.

RIGHT: Once war broke out, the Japanese attacks were merciless. This aerial view of Shanghai taken in August 1937 shows the devastation of the Business Centre after an air attack by the Japanese; at the front to the right is a stretch of the old racecourse, once a centre of Western social life. The towers at the back belonged to three famous department stores. *(Corbis U407358ACME Bettmann/CORBIS)*.

FAR RIGHT: In this horrific scene, bodies lie piled up on the streets after the Japanese bombed the city in September 1937 *(Corbis 42-17230341 Bettmann/Corbis)*.

A panoramic view of The Bund in 1937;
the Huangpu river is seen crowded with
fighting craft of many nations, including
Japanese boats, here seen bombarding the
Chinese area. A large, mysterious explosion
had occurred earlier in the day
(Corbis U604649INP Bettmann/CORBIS).

There was no wholesale destruction of foreign property; The Bund, that symbol of foreign dominance in Shanghai, is still largely unchanged externally, although many of the buildings have been re-cycled for use by Chinese organizations. The Shanghai Museum has been re-housed in a magnificent building in the People's Park, but close to it is the 1929 Mu'en Tang, an inter-denominational church where services are held in Chinese. Across the road, in the riverside gardens, (mainly elderly) Chinese citizens still exercise and socialize in the early morning.

There were signs of change, the most important being the establishment of Ningbo as a major container port, and the subsequent decrease in the importance of Shanghai as a port. But the main reason for the stagnation of the city was the Government's decision not to invest as generously in this already comparatively wealthy city, as it did in others, whose needs were possibly greater. It has been suggested that this may have been a political decision, resulting from Shanghai's long tradition as an independently-minded (potential) rival to Beijing. Whatever the reason, the city remained largely unchanged until the early 1990s, just before the handover of Hong Kong, when vast sums were invested in the city, so that it once more became one of the greatest and most glamorous cities in the world, attracting large numbers of overseas tourists.

LEFT: The ferocity of the Japanese attacks led to residents of the International settlement opening their gates to allow some Chinese to find safety; the Chinese refugee here is accompanied by a British Officer and two American Marines. In August 1937 the atmosphere was tense as Japanese warships threatened the city and Chinese forces prepared to defend it *(Corbis U381504INP Bettmann/Corbis)*.

ABOVE: When the Second World War broke out, the Japanese turned on the foreign residents; the streets were barricaded with barbed wire *(LoC 33559u)*.

LEFT: Once Japan was defeated, the Nationalist and Communist forces turned on each other. The city was a hotbed of unrest and fear as the Communist forces approached; this view of Suzhou Creek shows the great Astor House Hotel looking out over a harbour full of Chinese barges laden with goods, awaiting an uncertain future *(Corbis U375710INP Bettmann/Corbis).*

ABOVE: In May 1949 Nationalist troops marched into Shanghai to defend it from the Communists; five months later, Chiang Kai Shek had been defeated and the People's Republic of China was established *(Corbis U11131012INP Bettmann/Corbis).*

ABOVE: Brick houses were more substantial but crowded *(iStockphoto 4111202 winhorse)*.

FAR LEFT: In 1946 ships in the harbour included an American cruiser at anchor in the Huangpo River *(Corbis UKD506AINP Bettmann/Corbis)*.

CENTER LEFT: It was many years before Shanghai would recover; not until the early 1990s was much money invested in its modernization, so the last decade has seen a remarkable change in its appearance. The most dramatic building was perhaps the Soviet-style Exhibition Hall, built in 1954 at the height of Russian influence to celebrate the speed of technological change since the Communists came to power *(Fotolia 940830 Yunwn Yuan)*.

LEFT: Otherwise in the 1980s it was still very much as it had been for more than 30 years. Old streets were largely unchanged; back streets were narrow and the air-conditioner is a reminder that, although Shanghai had extremes in temperature, it—like other cities south of the Yellow River—had neither air-conditioning nor heating systems *(iStockphoto 1714361 Holger Bischoff)*.

LEFT: Streets were festooned with washing as there was nowhere else to dry clothes (*iStockphoto 4894035 Frank Van Den Berg*).

ABOVE: Even small local restaurants had no running hot water, and all drinking water had to be boiled and stored in flasks (*iStockphoto 3829871 winhorse*).

ABOVE: Nothing was wasted. Bicycles were still the most common form of transport *(iStockphoto 4053362 Chandra Menard).*

RIGHT: Behind the fire hydrant can be seen a typical mobile street night food stall, China's answer to the fast food craze *(iStockphoto 2504521 Robert Churchill).*

FAR LEFT: Local small craftsmen made tiles and bricks (iStockphoto 3872489 winhorse).

LEFT: Everything was recycled—and carried by pedicycle (iStockphoto 2361778 Lewis Muerig Jones).

ABOVE: At that time, tourists only seemed to comment on three things—squatter loos, the throwing of chicken bones on the floor, and frequent hawking and spitting. China was only just beginning to realize the value of tourism (iStockphoto 1664974 Tamir Niv).

These three images are typical of Shanghai street scenes in the mid-1980s:

ABOVE: A typical street scene *(Joan Waller)*.

RIGHT: You can enjoy a tour of Shanghai at a leisurely pace *(Joan Waller)*.

FAR RIGHT: Small shops displaying poor quality goods on the pavements—all scenes very different from today *(Joan Waller)*.

The Phoenix City

An aerial view of the busy Huangpu River which flows 110 kilometers from the Yangtze to the open sea and is the source of much of Shanghai's prosperity *(iStockphoto 4788138 Frank van den Berg)*.

The Phoenix City

In the 1980s, Shanghai was not only drab, neglected and falling behind other rapidly-expanding cities, but it also suffered from a very severe epidemic of hepatitis which led to its being isolated from the rest of China. This did not help it to regain its reputation as a tourist centre. But in the last two decades its transformation has been extraordinary. Whether this is because the Chinese Government wanted to promote it at the cost of Hong Kong in order to attract foreign business or was confident enough to decide that there was space for two great cities in mainland China isn't clear. What is certain is that the rise of Shanghai was closely related to the rise of a number of powerful and effective mayors and senior administrators in the city.

Symbols of Shanghai's leap into the twenty-first century are the Stock Exchange and the Formula One Racing Track, opened in 2005 and, in typical Shanghai style, combining traditional culture—it is said to represent the Chinese character shang, as in Shanghai, meaning "above"—with advanced technology.

In the main city, there has been vast investment in the public transport system. Its subway system is still being developed, but since the first line was opened in 1995, two others have been added. The system is clean, safe, cheap, and easy to follow—even for non-Chinese speakers. The new International Pudong Airport is linked to the subway at Longyang Lu by the high-tech Maglev train which

LEFT: The Lotus Tower is a dramatic
backdrop to one such site
(iStockphoto 4205091 Ludger Vorfeld).

ABOVE: The city was full of demolition sites
during the 1990s
(iStockphoto 4369421 alandj).

reaches speeds of 270 miles (430 kilometers) per hour, and takes only eight minutes to cover its 20-mile journey. Taxis too are cheap, and have meters installed, but, like buses, can take a long time to travel extensive distances because of traffic congestion. The road system has been modernized; the city is divided by expressways from East to West, with central access to the North-South Overhead Road. The surreal Bund Sightseeing Tunnel and the more mundane traffic tunnels linking Shanghai to Pudong are other examples of carefully planned projects.

Several sites have been developed as attractive and well-maintained parks. The most famous is the People's Park, developed from the old Racecourse, and is now not only a popular meeting place, but a superb setting for the great Shanghai Museum, opened in 1995, based on the shape of an antique cooking pot, the elegant glass Museum of Contemporary Art, the Urban Planning Exhibition Centre with its complex angular roof, and the Grand Theatre, with its roof (a great curve over glass walls). There are many other spectacular new buildings on the mainland, but close by are still some much more traditional glimpses of an older Shanghai—washing lines criss-crossing narrow streets, flea markets with dusty relics of a pre-Communist life, stalls of handicrafts and fresh vegetables and old women teetering along in tiny shoes.

It is across the river in Pudong that the most dramatic changes have occurred.

Said to be Pudong's finest skyscraper at 421 meters (1,379 feet), Jinmao Tower is a vast complex of offices, shops, a hotel and viewing gallery; its distinctive silver pillar narrows to a fine point, like a pen

112

LEFT: The contrast between old and new is startling
(*Fotolia 4348309 vanostaeyen&demunynck*).

ABOVE: There are many interesting contrasts between old and new buildings; here Chinese houses contrast with high rise blocks
(*iStockphoto 1699200 Holger Bischoff*).

RIGHT: The old Shanghai Art Museum is dwarfed by modern skyscrapers
(*Fotolia 4638370 vanostaeyen&demunynck*)

nib. At its foot are the curving roof of the Exhibition Hall and, not far away, the instantly identifiable Oriental Pearl TV Tower, its slender structure like a space rocket about to take off from a great globe of a launch-pad. The Shanghai Ocean Aquarium, rated one of the best in the world, is famous for its underwater viewing tunnels, stretching for nearly 150 meters (500 feet). And in Century Square, along with local government buildings, there is a giant sculpture signifying time, as well as the Oriental Arts Center, shaped like the city's flower, the magnolia—yet another example of Shanghai's desire to preserve its own cultural links.

Two of the longest double suspension bridges in the world—Nanpu Bridge and Yangpu Bridge—link Pudong with the mainland, and, along with the Orient Pearl TV Tower, have already entered the world of Chinese myth with the title "Two Dragons playing with the Pearl"; they are a spectacular sight at night.

Pudong has become one of the greatest trading centres of the world, but now Shanghai faces the problem of how to house the thousands of well-off professionals, both Chinese and foreign, financial and academic, who have settled in the city. Its answer is typically Shanghaiese—"One City, Nine Towns". And, despite the increase in cheaper housing, there are signs that the gap between the rich and the poor in Shanghai, as in the rest of China, is increasing. It will be interesting to see how it copes with the issue.

RIGHT: Skyscrapers dominate a traditional pavilion (iStockphoto 187320 Mat Tsz Fung).

LEFT: In Downtown Shanghai old European buildings stand out against modern skyscrapers (*Fotolia 5373380 PhotoAlex*).

ABOVE: There are still remnants of old Shanghai to be seen; some back streets still look as they did before Shanghai was modernized (*Fotolia 442070 Catherine Perarnard*).

FAR LEFT: Old people gather in the street to play "Go" *(Fotolia 2260031 morane)*.

LEFT: You can still find prayer stones *(Fotolia 3961430 vanostaeyen&demunynck)*.

ABOVE: People exercising in the early morning on The Bund use traditional red silk fans *(iStockphoto 2656824 Robert Churchill)*.

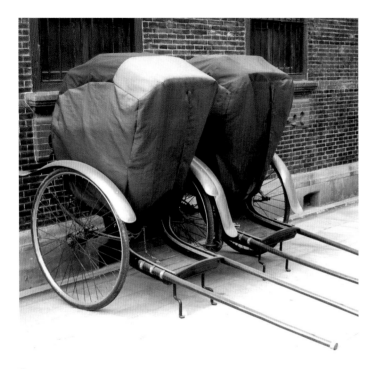

ABOVE: And rickshaws are still available for hire—although now they are used by tourists
(iStockphoto 187235 Mak Tsz Fung).

RIGHT: There has been some sensitive restoration of earlier work such as this Art Deco door
(iStockphoto 3920630 Terraxplorer).

LEFT: The summit of this skyscraper seems to echo the Art Deco style *(Fotolia 5203540 Ude Ingber)*.

ABOVE: It is sometimes hard to tell if a building has been restored, as at the Yu Yuan Gardens *(iStockphoto 4793274 Frank van den Berg)*.

RIGHT: In Xintiandi, in what was once the French Concession, traditional Shikumen or stone door houses have been refurbished and many converted into elegant shops and restaurants, with pavement cafes *(iStockphoto 2179705 Zhang Xiao Qiu)*.

FAR RIGHT: Sometimes the alterations are not so tactful, as in this garden pool with its enormous lotus flowers *(Fotolia 2118666 Hermann Marka)*.

OVERLEAF: Lighting has been used very effectively; the view of The Bund by day is transformed at night *(iStockphoto 4310215 Terraxplorer)*.

ABOVE: Lighting adds glamour to individual buildings such as the Hong Kong and Shanghai Bank and the Customs House on The Bund *(Fotolia 5018460 Jonathan Larsen).*

RIGHT: Or emphasizes the silhouette of a traditional tea-house *(iStockphoto 401394 Youssouf Cader).*

LEFT AND ABOVE: New buildings are
similar to those in Hong Kong, with
forests of skyscrapers such as these in
Downtown Shanghai
*(iStockphoto 4667149 Holger Mette;
iStockphoto 2689978 Robert Churchill).*

But, some apparently traditional skyscrapers have unusual details, such as this one with a "plaited" roof *(Fotolia 719297 Martha Bayona).*

RIGHT: And this one with a wheel on top *(Fotolia 4198986 vanostaeyen&demunnynek).*

ABOVE: Many of the most striking new buildings are either in the People's Park and Square built on what was once the old racecourse in central Shanghai *(iStockphoto 2118212 Zhang Xiao Qiu).*

RIGHT: Innovative new buildings and parks have added light and colour to the city *(iStockphoto 4431839 Loic Bernard).*

LEFT: The service in restaurants has improved greatly *(Joan Waller)*.

ABOVE: At favourite sites such as the Yu Yuan Bazaar there are plenty of souvenir shops and fast food outlets *(Joan Waller)*.

RIGHT: At the spectacular Grand Theatre there are superb performances, both Chinese and Western
(Fotolia 940136 Yuanwu Yuan).

RIGHT: Not all visitors like genuine Chinese dishes but dim sum is a favourite with nearly everyone *(Fotolia 3426623 Bertrand Benoit).*

But there is something for everyone from FAR RIGHT: Formula One racing to OVERLEAF LEFT & CENTER museums, shopping to

OVERLEAF RIGHT: sky jumping *(Joan Waller; Joan Waller; Fotolia 2701172 Xof711).*

LEFT: There are plenty of "antique" shops, but many items are reproductions; you cannot take genuine antiques out of China unless they carry a seal *(Fotolia 3553710 Rene Drouyer).*

RIGHT: Because life in Shanghai changes so quickly, what you see today you may never see again—unlike Christmas *(Fotolia 2260049 morane).*

The Future?
One City, Nine Towns

Pudong by night; demolition is rapidly being overtaken by construction; today Shanghai is said to have the greatest number of cranes in operation of any city in the world *(Fotolia 5760283 Holger Mette).*

The Future? One City, Nine Towns

In what seems an ironic reversal of its past history, but which suggests the increasing self-confidence of China as a whole, Shanghai has turned to foreign expertize as well as to foreign architecture to help it provide housing for the new generation of migrants and expats who have flooded into the city in the past ten years. Costing billions of yuan, these satellite towns are not purely dormitory towns; each one has a specific theme—education, the car industry—which links residents to a particular country and so to the style of architecture employed. The nine countries involved are those which had a significant impact on the city's earlier history.

Organized by the Urban Planning Institute, the projects are overseen by the City Council, but designed by foreign architects: Gregotti Associati International are responsible for the first, Pujiang, which, like many older cities both in China and Italy, is based upon a grid. It will be the largest of the nine towns, and will reflect the varied usage of the area on the other side of the river—tourism, leisure, commerce and housing. It is expected that this first stage of the project will be completed during 2009–14; the German and the British towns are already under construction, and they will be followed by the other six—the United States, Russia, Spain, Sweden, France and the Netherlands.

The site was originally agricultural land criss-crossed by canals; the architect has preserved the past as much as possible by the use

FAR LEFT AND LEFT: Surprisingly to many Westerners, bamboo is still used for scaffolding because of its cheapness, strength and durability
(Fotolia 5204686 Udo Ingber; iStockphoto 603700 Andrew Wood).

of bridged canals set with trees, plenty of open green spaces, cycle tracks and low-rise buildings. As in traditional Chinese dwellings, there are internal courtyards and, as in Italy, there is a palazzo set on an island in a lake. So often, the Chinese have demonstrated their ability to take ideas from foreign sources and make them their own.

At Anting, a village to the West of Shanghai, a totally different town is being built, based upon the German town of Weimar; its buildings are a vivid terracotta, its terrace blocks rising to six or seven storeys. Wide streets, a Volkswagen factory and a Formula One racetrack are only three of the factors which suggest its theme—the automobile.

The UK is represented by Thames Town—an "Olde English Town" in Songjiang, complete with Tudor timbering and Victorian red brick, with turreted castle and Catholic cathedral, not to mention pubs, football pitches and markets. It is planned to accommodate 8,000 residents, mostly university teachers and factory managers, and planners hope to attract newly-affluent Chinese as well as foreigners. In addition there will be nine universities, a huge shopping mall, and factories built for hi-tech firms such as Hitachi offering employment.

Initial enthusiasm for the project may be waning; there has been less promotion of it in the media, and mounting criticism. High costs, property prices ($490,000 is the minimum price for villas in a city where the average annual earning is $2,700) and a feeling that this reliance upon foreign design is not in keeping with Shanghai's status as China's second city, all play their part. As Chinese national confidence increases, there is a fear that too many other cities in the

FAR LEFT: Jinmao Tower, designed by the American architects Skidmore, Owings and Merrill, and rising to 1,380 feet (421 meters), is said to be the finest in Pudong *(iStockphoto 3594771 Chandra Menard)*.

LEFT: Here it is under construction *(iStockphoto 4667132 Holger Mette)*.

ABOVE: Its interior is as breath-taking as its exterior; it has 88 storeys, with the Grand Hyatt Hotel occupying the 53rd to the 87th floors and a hollow core which allows for a vertiginous view of the different levels *(iStockphoto 4382809 alandj)*.

country may follow Shanghai's example, so detracting from China's own ancient heritage. Above all, planners are beginning to realize that, unless more affordable housing is made available, there could be serious social unrest in the city.

It will be interesting to see how this great city responds to the challenges which lie ahead.

FAR LEFT: The whole skyline of Pudong is magnificent whether seen from The Bund in daylight
(Fotolia 3197718 jiongkai zhang).

LEFT: Or by night, when the Lotus Tower adds even more to its splendour
(iStockphoto 2681997 photomorphic).

FAR LEFT: Other memorable buildings include Shanghai Museum, based on the shape of an ancient Chinese bronze *(Fotolia 3551296 Rene Drouyer).*

LEFT: The Grand Theatre with its concave roof and glass walls from which there is a spectacular view of the city lights *(iStockphoto 2150922 Zhang Xiao Qiu).*

LEFT: The Exhibition Centre with its four corner pinnacles *(Corbis 42-18156026 Marc Gerritsen/Arcaid/Corbis).*

ABOVE: And the East sculpture in Century Square *(Fotolia 3553952 Rene Drouyer).*

FAR LEFT: Although not so dramatic, the contrast between different forms of housing is illuminating; in the past, even apartment blocks were comparatively low rise as there were no lifts, and each work unit had its own standard housing, so no job meant no housing. But now many people can afford to buy a house or apartment, and these suburban low rise houses are definitely for the better-off
(Fotolia 940988 Yanwu Yuan).

LEFT: In some areas low and high rise contrast
(iStockphoto 4417217 Olav Wildermann).

ABOVE: Some high rise housing is still very high density
(iStockphoto 3739932 Earl Eliason).

RIGHT: But some is surrounded by parkland and there is a movement away from the ubiquitous grey of earlier housing *(iStockphoto 630362 Irwan Soetkno).*

FAR RIGHT: On the other hand some look like battery farming *(iStockphoto 4344442 Hakan Aldrin).*

LEFT: The first Maglev train in the world runs from Shanghai Central to Pudong International Airport at a speed of up to 500 kilometers per hour *(Fotolia 5760528 Holger Motte)*.

Vast improvements in transport benefit both locals and tourists although cars, despite attempts to limit their numbers, are a problem, as in Downtown Shanghai *(Fotolia 4288147 Jim Pickerell).*

Traffic congestion has led to the building of aerial roads *(Fotolia 342205 Dennis Reich).*

FAR LEFT: And enormous roundabouts
(iStockphoto 4551308 George Clerk).

LEFT: Taxis whose drivers were once a law
unto themselves are now carefully regulated
(iStockphoto 1247358 Chee Woon Peng).

LEFT: There is a city-wide efficient Metro service; this is the entry to The Bund metro station *(Fotolia 940977 Yanwu YUAN)*.

LEFT: And both railway services and stations, such as Shanghai South, have been much improved *(Fotolia 3575301 Lily Forman)*.

Index